25th April 2005

GW01466404

Dear !

Thank you for your
support for this.

You have done (are
doing) so much
for Nikki + Charlie.

I hope you enjoy
the poems.

Best wishes from

Phil.
xx

Blades of Grass

*(forty-four original published poems
and six published poems in translation)*

Philip Dunkerley

Dedicated to the memory of Steve Cawte

For family and friends - the people who really matter.
Also for Rio - the inspiration for the title poem
and star of the cover photo.

Woof woof !

First Edition

Published in 2025 by Serena Books
e-mail: **dunkerleyphilip@hotmail.com**

ISBN 978-1-4452-5241-4

Design by Serena Books

Produced in Great Britain via lulu.com

Contents   Page

Preface

This is my third collection of poems which have all appeared previously in editor-moderated magazines, webzines or anthologies - in this case a total of 44 of my own poems plus six of my translations of poems into English from either Spanish or Portuguese. So, a total of 50 poems to add to the 51 in *As Red as Rubies* and the 49 of *Schrödinger's Eco-Cat*.

Is it legitimate to include translations with my own poems? Well, it's been said that a poem in translation is a new poem, and I'll go into that in a little more detail in the introduction to Section Two of the collection, which is where the translated poems appear.

Section One is where my own poems are, placed pretty much in the order that they were accepted for publication. Information intended to aid an appreciation of the poems can be found in the Endnotes.

Last year, in July, I enjoyed a get-together with one of my poetry friends, Richard Horne, who has serious heart issues, and another such friend, Steve Cawte, who had actually undergone a heart transplant at Papworth Hospital in Cambridge, less than three months before. Sadly, Steve died on August 21st while this book was in preparation. As the three of us discussed, and as supported by Nikki, Steve's wife, the full proceeds from the sale of up to 100 copies of *Blades of Grass*, and / or any additional sales of *As Red as Rubies* and *Schrödinger's Eco-Cat*, will be donated to Papworth Hospital charities, in aid of heart disease.

For me, poetry is the deepest way we can use language, and it is language that makes us human. Also, it is my belief that poems should be both understandable and enjoyable and I hope that the contents of the following pages will achieve both these aims.

If you would like to contact me about any of the poems, please do so via the e-mail address shown on the Copyright page.

Steve Cawte

Steven Robert Cawte was born on November 8th 1982 and died on August 21st 2024, aged only 41. He was a multi-talented man, describing himself as a *Poet, Playwright, Actor, Host, Director and Educator*. In fact, he was much more. He lived in Lincoln with his wife and two teenage children. To the end, he was energetic, productive, supportive of others and loved life.

My first contact with Steve was in mid-2019 when he and Shirley Bell set up *Impspired*, initially as a poetry webzine. Not long after, Shirley had to drop out, because of ill-health, and Steve continued as sole editor, quickly developing *Impspired* into an independent publishing house. By 2022, when Steve issued the poetry anthology *Love, Loss and Cardiac Issues*, I knew he had serious health problems, but it was only by consulting Facebook posts in June 2024 that I understood how serious; Steve had received a heart transplant at Papworth Hospital at the end of April, just two months before.

Together with Richard, a fellow-member of Bourne U3A Poetry Group, I met Steve at *The Centurion* pub in North Hykeham on 25th July. There we found a quiet table and talked hearts and poetry over a good lunch.

As I was hoping to publish *Blades of Grass*, we discussed donating some of the proceeds to Papworth, to where Richard is in the process of transferring his case. Both Steve and he said they would support the launch event, which I hoped could happen in Stamford Arts Centre, my 'local' poetry venue. Papworth got behind the project and on 22nd August I e-mailed Steve to update him on progress, telling him I'd sent the collection off for printing of a proof copy. However, my e-mail was too late and under the circumstances, with Nikki's support, the collection is now dedicated to Steve's memory.

Steve was a fantastic human being, full of energy, empathy, ambition and life - in that broad, human, sense of the word.

Section One: Forty-four Published Poems

Saying Goodbye

Published in Impspired #31, February 2025 [1]

Elegy for Steve Cawte - re. 21st August 2024

Beauty is truth, truth beauty—that is all you need to know
— John Keats

I found out only later you were leaving -
I thought you'd still be with us, going on.
It was evening, I was walking home, alone,
and feeling sad because the swifts had gone.

I miss the swifts of summer, they, for me,
are truth writing beauty on the sky,
and I sometimes feel an emptiness inside
knowing I'll lose that beauty when I die.

Suddenly, looking up, there, overhead,
a familiar silhouette in swinging flight,
a last, lone swift - as if saying goodbye,
a spectacle in early evening light.

All of us will one day say goodbye,
all of us will leave the world behind,
the beauty and the truth; you left too soon.
You, who were the best of humankind.

3

Advice to a Friend on His Retirement

Published in Pennine Platform, #92, 2022 [2]
for John Graydon

When you don't know your *Cumulus congestus* from your
Stratus fractus,
when you've finished with the fray and it's time for a different
dream,
when the green space that leads down to the stream
is the space that calls to you, and you look up at the sky
and begin to wonder about the clouds - *Low*, *Medium* and *High*

you'll need to learn the terminology;
find a good book, keep it close, learn about meteorology
and the atmosphere of our planet of green and blue,
the thin air of the clouds, and what they get up to.

Sins of Emission

Published in The Seventh Quarry, #38, 2023 [3]

Saying 'No' to Carbon Taxes

The abundant sparrows of my childhood
are deconstructed now. Those words
'You don't know what you've got
til it's gone' re-echo in my mind.

We cannot all go north where ice
sweats from the backs of ancient gneiss,
or south where endless canopies of green
once clothed our vital planet.

We sit and watch the moving scenes,
transfusions of hard facts into our veins,
naked rock, bare bones of earth, wounds
crying to be covered over once again.

Meanwhile, facing the wrong direction,
those who will not hear the pleas,
who fail to write the words that might
allow our home to heal and breathe.

Swallow Tale

Published in The Seventh Quarry, #38, 2023 [4]

'Swallows certainly sleep all winter. A number of them conglobulate
together, by flying round and round, and then all in a heap throw
themselves under water, and lye in the bed of a river.'
            — Samuel Johnson (1709-1784)

Science says swallows migrate each autumn
to Africa. Once, though, people thought
they dived into rivers, burying themselves
in mud, hibernating till the spring arrived.

Today, a quiet September afternoon,
walking along a footpath near the village,
I watched the swallows looping and turning
over ancient fields of ridge and furrow.
And then I thought: *If you believe the folklore*
they'll be readying themselves to take the plunge.

There's a sort of strange appeal in tradition -
those medieval workers who trudged out
each day, come rain or shine, to tend the land,
surely they must have known a thing or two?

Just then I heard a twittering sound and turned
in time to see, wheeling past the windmill,
and heading south, a flock of flying hedgehogs.

Springtime on Harrington Street

Published in Lighten-Up Online (LUPO), #61, 2023 [5]

I was walking one morning down Harrington Street, in Bourne,
in Lincolnshire,
it was springtime with flowers and a warmth in the air as the
sun spread a feeling of cheer,
so I started to muse on the earth and its bounty, and how it all
came about,
and my thoughts went back to time out of mind when nothing
is certain but doubt.

Four billion years ago, scientists say, stuck in goo was a
carbony cell
that managed to copy itself exactly and did it remarkably well.
It did it so well that it did it again, without any struggle or strife,
and now to that moment, so long ago, we attribute the start of
Life!

Each cell produced could do the same thing, and soon there
were plenty about,
but sometimes the process went slightly awry, and new types
began to come out.
Each type was a species, and each type set out to maximise
its distribution,
and thus, in a very small way, in the sea, life started on
Evolution.

When half a billion years had gone by, some species were
clearly superior,
and the best of the lot, spread all over the place, were those
that we call the bacteria.
They'd worked out a trick that was ever so clever - some would
say almost *parfait* -
of passing on secrets of how to make copies - encoded in DNA.

It was not very long before life discovered that it needed food to survive,
and eating your neighbour was quite a good way of ensuring that you stayed alive.
So *'kill or be killed'* was a lesson bacteria taught to their offspring with care,
and *'look out for yourself'* was further advice they wanted descendants to share.

The name of the game was to keep going on, reproducing in each generation,
and passing your DNA on down the line in a process of self-replication.
If ever you failed to continue the chain of life, or in some way unlinked,
then that was the end, kaput, goodbye, you simply became extinct.

At that time the earth's atmosphere was austere and oxygen gas was a blight
but then some bacteria made the world cheerier by making their food from sunlight.
The work was frenetic, and photosynthetic, and these species' faeces, I swear,
emitted O^2 as gas in their poo, and that made a breath of fresh air.

The above took place at the end of the time that geologists call the Archaean
and life successfully prospered and thrived because it was tough and protean.
By now we have got to two billion years (or so) in the past - time flies,
and worms and bizarre squidgy squalachy things were starting to be of some size.

This part of earth history is usually known by the name of 'the Proterozoic',
and plants and animals strove to adapt in ways that were truly heroic.
Each living thing could trace its descent right back to that carbony cell,
their bodies were soft, they didn't have bones, and neither a carbonate shell.

At somewhere around five hundred and forty two million years ago changes
of early (Precambrian) species occurred, filling more niches and ranges.
For example, the limpets, with tough little shells, appeared spreading farther and nearer,
today we can find them as fossils in limestones denoting the Cambrian era.

It wasn't long after that vertebrates flourished, like sharks, which persist to this day
- this was in Ordovician times, and Silurian too, so they say.
And then there appeared the ancestors of fish such as sea-horses, eels and trout,
and others with such unpronounceable names, that I think that I'll just leave them out.

Well now we have reached the Devonian era with deserts all over the place,
and then in the Carboniferous period forests of ferns grew apace
- they gave us our coal, and crawling about in the forests, the swamps and the bogs
there were cute little animals getting along that later gave rise to the frogs.

I don't want to imply that the sole way to die before reproducing was falling...
as prey to some animal bigger than you - a fate that was simply appalling,
for mass-extinctions occurred now and then, perhaps if the climate changed fast,
or somewhere a mighty volcano went off dealing death with the force of the blast.

But life is exuberant, never says die, and after disaster moves on
evolving new species well-able to cope and replace former ones that have gone.
And the chains from the carbony cell continued and link after link they'd make,
and frogs and their kind saw appear on the continents crocodile, tortoise and snake.

After the coal swamps had come and had gone, Permo-Triassic time came,
and deserts, once more, covered much of the land, so survival was quite a tough game.
But then the Jurassic got going, and earth saw the dinosaurs reaching their prime,
and snakes and frogs, and other small animals, had to lie low for a time.

It was when the great dinosaurs wandered the earth that the forebears of mammals appeared
- they lived underground, emerging at night, because they were small and afeared.
Perhaps they were friendly with frogs and their ilk - or perhaps they competed for space.
Froggy hopped on as the mammals sped off to give rise to the human race.

The time when the White Cliffs of Dover were formed is a period called the Cretaceous,
it began with the bang of a meteorite impact that wiped out some species - good gracious!
It did for the dinosaurs, birds though survived, and happily too so did mammals,
and they quickly evolved, producing new species like mammoths and fruit bats and camels.

Sixty-five million years ago marks the the start of Tertiary time when the world took on a familiar look as mammals came into their prime.
But everything living - from monkeys to worms and bees and bacteria too
are linkages made of the unbroken chains that go back to the carbony goo.

So just to remind us, if ever there'd been a break in the sequence of life
that's been going along for ever, it seems, through chaos, convulsion and strife,
we wouldn't be here, not us nor the grass, the flowers, the oak or the pine,
and if we don't propagate while we still can, then that is the end of the line.

Let's take an example and look at the frog. A frog you see hopping today
can only exist because *all* of its ancestors passed on their DNA;
it goes back to that carbony cell in the goo, four billions of years in the past,
and unless froggy mates to continue the chain, then his link will now be the last.

And as I was musing I saw a fine frog hopping out from a
garden gate,
he was heading across to a pond in the park, and hoping to
find him a mate.
He hopped off the kerb and into the road, eager for love and
romance -
and that's when a Mini came speeding along, and the bugger
stood never a chance!

As froggy came quick to the end of the line, so quickly I'm
ending my story.
I know for the squeamish that squashing of frogs may perhaps
seem excessively gory.
But the business of life is brutish and short and froggy was
slow on his feet,
and that's why his genes became smithereens, besplattered
on Harrington Street!

Black Gold

Published in Acumen, #105, 2023 [6]

Lynemouth, Northumberland

After the storm in the night
the sea comes washing in
like the swirl of the miner's pan,
sifting, separating, stranding.

Dark tidemarks
along the lap of the beach;
bright nuggets of coal
released from the ribs of the earth,
black gold, a gift from the deep.

Night Flight

Published in South Poetry, #67, 2023 [7]

When you're done with the day's worrying
about the plight of humanity, feeling concern
that the bedrock of our existence is heaving,

you go for a walk into the dark night
through the empty town, a few stars shining.
You're alone on silent streets wrapped up

against the cold. And you hear a noise, far off,
like a barking of dogs through the clear air,
which you disregard, until you realise

that it's getting closer. Suddenly you know,
with complete certainty, that it's geese,
and you see them above the houses, coming,

urging each other on, until here they are,
thirty or forty, a wide and shallow skein,
flying low, flying resolutely onwards.

What must they make of this lighted mosaic,
street lamps illuminating them, turning them
ghost-grey, making of them unearthly beings?

It's the juxtaposition of human hopelessness
and the wild freedom of the geese flying away.
You stand, listening to their fading calls, gone.

Quarry (disused)

Published in Obsessed with Pipework, #102, 2023 [8]

the stone of the place became the place of the town
the taking of the stone was the making of the place
the making of the town was the placing of the stone
the empty place is witness to the making of the town

the emptiness of place is the stone of the town
the birth of the town was the breaking of the stone
the breaking of the stone was the spoiling of the place
the spoil of the place was the winning of the stone

the empty place is strange to the people of the town
the open place an empty space of ragged broken ground
the strange place gave the town the story of its stone
the story of the town is a crowded stony place

the people fill the quiet place each with a stone
the stones tell stories in the cold and silent ground

Crow Triolet

Published in Snakeskin, #302, 2022 [9]

Out in the wilderness, silent the snow
- glaring, immaculate, perfectly white -
flurry of feathers, there landed a Crow
out in the wilderness
                              (silent the snow).
Sudden intruder, he came like a foe,
blacker than calumny, darker than night,
out in the wilderness, silent the snow,
glaring, immaculate, perfectly white.

Blades of Grass

Published in The Lake, June 2023 [10]

I bequeath myself to the dirt to grow from the grass I love,
if you want me again look for me under your boot-soles.
          — Walt Whitman, 'Leaves of Grass'

Crouching here on the ragged edge
of this harrowed field,
my dog running on beyond the oak tree,
I take in my hands the dark earth,
soil of the planet of which I am part.

Earth, soil, soiling my hands.
From you, life, in you, the archive of life,
rich elegy of all that came before.
From you my forebears wrested a living,
your darkness their lives.

Like seeds we blow over the land
until, finding a place to put down roots,
we stay, living as best we might,
passing the germ of our selves on.
And, when we are done, we return,
dried-out blades of grass,
into this dark soil. We came at dawn,
like time capsules, unstoppable,
driven to make shift where we could,
unending chains of exuberance.

Now here am I fingering the earth,
the high clouds of heaven above;
and look! here is my amiable dog
jolting me back to the present.
Oh, Dog! Must I think for us both?

Reading with Kids

Published in The Lincolnshire Poacher, Summer 2023 [11]

Each week I go to Westfield School
to hear the children read,
the aim is to improve their
insight, fluency and speed.

I work with Mrs Bloomer's class,
of thirty kids or so,
I have a list of all their names
and mark it as we go.

They take their turn to bring the book
selected by themselves,
from thousands in the library,
on colour-coded shelves.

Side by side we sit and, if
it's needed, I explain
the tricky words and phrases that
all books, it seems, contain.

I tell the kids that each new word
they learn will be a friend,
that's always there to help them
and on whom they can depend.

So what's the pay-back for my time?
It's this: if children learn
to love to read, the way I do,
then that's a fair return.

Mountain

Published in The Cannon's Mouth, # 88, 2023 [12]

This mountain has made its own contours,
it has interpolated between the spot heights on its flanks.
It has decided what shape it will be when seen from space,
or a plane, or through the eyes of a buzzard flying above.

This mountain has drawn parallel lines across its screes
and thrown a welter of curves over its north-facing crags.
This mountain has traced v-shaped ravines for its streams,
two run eastwards into the lake, three go west to the sea.

This mountain has made a rock profile like a face
that has turned and looked over its shoulder.
It has craned its neck so it can observe the town,
it has pushed out spurs down to the coast.

This mountain has thought to make places for farms
and sheep folds, and sheltered them with sycamore trees.
This mountain is losing itself, stone by stone to the valley;
it resolutely opposes planning consent for a quarry.

Loss in Old Age

Published in The Cannon's Mouth, # 88, 2023 [13]

Pervasive emptiness wherever he looked,
outside into the green and blue beyond
or at every item of home, each marked
by moments of choice and of use.

And pervasive emptiness within. Those
relentless days of caring and comforting,
doing whatever he could - duty and love.
Knowing how but not when it would end.

What could a man do, now, to carry on?
How could a small future begin to build
against the immensity of time elapsed,
of the loss of half of what he had been?

Yet, when all choice becomes no choice,
living becomes, again, the end in itself.
Cold, clear water still waits to be drawn
from the depths of the well of the world.

Torn Away

Published in The Alchemy Spoon, #10, Summer 2023 [14]

in memory of José Francisco [Leopoldino] Filho

On looking back, memory is mainly gaps, like water running
between stepping stones,
and now that he's gone, the moment when we first met no
longer really exists.
There are only the struts and spars of our relationship - on
which hung patches and tatters
that, nevertheless, always had, when seen from a distance, a
semblance of friendship.

But there really was a moment, an actual encounter, when our
eyes met for the first time.
What did he make of me - unknown, different? What did I
make of him? I don't remember.
Thereafter, chance and sporadic meetings, conversations
when we respected the niceties,
each of us making context, getting along, avoiding friction,
trying to work each other out.

Of course we'd always have known, had we stopped to think,
that there would be an end,
that a day would come when half of everything would be torn
utterly away and lost.
Who could say which way it would go and who would be left to
draw conclusions?
That's a question whose answer, too late, I imagine he
probably worked out for himself.

Day Off

Published in Ink, Sweat and Tears (IS&T), 2023 [15]

Vultures don't fly on Sundays,
it's their day off.
No use saying you'd like to see them
flying about, they won't do it,
haven't for ages.

I can tell you where they are -
they're down by the disused railway
hanging out, walking up and down
in an ungainly way,
talking about this and that -
subjects of vulture interest.

Some of them play cards
and board games
to stop them getting bored
- see what I did there?
I'm told that *'Disarticulate'*
is a current favourite.

One thing's sure,
they never cheat
- wouldn't want to get themselves
a bad name.

And the rubbish? It can rot.
They don't care.
They're not particularly religious,
but surely, after soaring about
the sky six days a week
looking for filth to eat,
you're entitled to a day off?

Waiting Area
Published in New Contexts: 5, an anthology, 2023 [16]

Quiet like peace, space like silence.
A sleek black dream machine stands
road-ready in the corner.
A man, fish-like, noses round it,
a salesman watches, patient as any angler.
The coffee is good - and it's free.
I assume someone's delving, prying,
checking, changing; my prepaid service.

Somewhere, there is music,
somewhere, the patter of speech;
outside the sun is shining.
I take up my book and time,
like a trail, heads off into the distance.
I read until this phrase catches my mind:
'the frolic of the early marriage bed'.
It arrests me. I am suddenly gone.

Us, there, back then, our meetings,
our blood hot with desire.
Frolic I think, *yes, it was like that…*
wherever we were, it was always like that.
I'm paging through memories
when the receptionist suddenly appears
with my car keys, smiling,
thinking she's doing the right thing.

Picasso the Communist - Me Neither

Published in The Journal, #70, 2023 [17]

in memory of Pablo Picasso, d. 8/4/1973

The programme on my car radio,
and I alone in the dark, crossing
the massive black blocks of the
fissile mountains, a moonscape
empty of life. The road unrolling
under my wheels, the world too.
I had only to steer, left and right.

Dead, they said, at ninety-one
- the man with so many names -
his old body slouched in the back
of my car; I could feel the drag
of his strong hands on the wheel,
his need for a beautiful woman -
a fresh Muse for every new mood.

I became a part of the night, lifted
backwards across the decades,
the Later, the War, the Surreal
- the even tones of a man's voice
from the speaker - Cubism,
Primitivism, the Rose and the Blue.
I was there in every moment.

When we came to Guernica,
the symbolism which has no words,
the SS man barked *Who did that,
was it you?* and Picasso retorted
No, it was you! The road unrolling,
me, lost in the dark, the sound filling
the air waves, reaching all parts.

Stranger in a Strange Land

Published in The Journal, #70, 2023 [18]

Who is this man sitting alone on a bench
near the church, a big man, long blond hair;
a Viking eating his lunch, a petrol-driven
lawnmower parked beside him?

Who is this big man walking the streets,
old combat jacket, ex-army backpack,
black trousers tied with string at the ankles,
cheap black boots, and his lawnmower?

Who is this silent man, with the long stride,
toting his rattling machine, like a toy,
incongruously around the town,
like something from Terry Street?

Who is this man in someone's front garden
sweeping up leaves, the householder
talking to him, but he does not stop
what he's doing, like he's on a mission?

Who is this one-time soldier standing alone
at the town cenotaph, behind the crowd,
remembering Helmand, tears in his eyes
as a young cadet massacres the Last Post ?

In Transit

Published in London Grip, 2023 [19]

him not there   her   & her girls
rabat   an alien culture   alone
three no-ones   in their eyes

because of   an   interpretation
a seventh - century text   men
having   to be out   by twelve noon

them stuck in the foyer   8 hours
to kill   two little ones   tired
looking daggers   because

of   a book   and   man power
because   they   could   8 hours
tired   feeding   nappies   mess

her   determined   but them
knowing   finally   the plane
would come   disdaining her

contempt   defiance   jack-knifed
worlds   them stuck in the past

disrespect   since he wasn't there

Darwin

Published in Lighten Up Online (LUPO), #64, 2023 [20]

I've heard a lot of nonsense about how life began,
it talks of evolution and about a certain man
whose name, they say, was Darwin; he'd a really bushy beard.
Well, clearly anyone like that is absolutely weird.

I don't believe in Darwin, I don't think he exists,
he's just a figment of the mind of evil scientists.
You can look him up on Google, but do not be deceived,
a lot of stuff on Google simply cannot be believed.

This Darwin chap, they'll tell you, wrote a book that's quite important
The Origin of Species; you can read it, but you oughtn't.
Me, I don't know anyone who's read the thing right through
but supporters of his theory think it's proven and it's true.

Although nobody reads the book, scientists all quote it
and think that Darwin wrote a sort of gospel when he wrote it.
They argue and they reason till they're running out of breath
but it's all a lot of rubbish and it bores me half to death.

It's outrageous that so many schools are teaching evolution
since common sense suggests it shows a mental destitution.
As anyone with half a brain will quickly understand
blind chance could never make an eye, a liver or a hand.

Evolutionists expect us to accept unlikely things
like gills becoming jaw bones, or lizards growing wings,
and claim that whales and hippos could be cousins once removed.
If you can prove such stuff, it shows that nonsense can be proved.

You may not like the mother of your Missus but admit
that, however unattractive, she doesn't look a bit
like a monkey that might jabber or go swinging in a tree
so she cannot be descended from an ape or chimpanzee.

Do not be led astray by the drivel that is bleated
by Darwinists who're desperate to win but are defeated.
They're wrong, and all Creationists are well aware of this:
The Origin of Species is the *Book of Genesis*.

Remembrance

Published in London Grip, 2023 [21]

He might well be from Terry Street, but isn't,
a Viking with long blond hair and cheapo boots.
He's cutting the green grass, green like Helmand,
laying neat stripes, marking a safe way home.

Summer's ending. Soon no one will want him.
Still he goes trudging about the town
pushing, incongruously, his petrol lawn mower,
looking for work, trying to keep control.

November now, and see, he's there again,
old combat jacket, wool hat, busy weeding.
It's a long way down for such a big-boned man,
but he's grateful to have any job at all.

And killing weeds is good - destroying them,
or eradicating pests - like on a mission.
They got the others. Somehow he survived.
But still he keeps them with him, in his head.

Remembrance Day, the Cenotaph, he's there,
alone, behind the crowd, tears in his eyes.
And then a kid cadet butchers the *'Last Post'*.
In the wounded silence, everything explodes.

Hobson

Published in Strix, #11, 2024 [22]

She'd wanted a dog; serendipity intervened.
The rescue centre, a friendly stray cat.
She took him.

Fed him on Pedigree Chum.
He went along with it - couldn't read -
Hobson's choice.

They were good for each other,
made the best of it, mutual benefit,
accommodation.

Sometimes she let him sit on her knee.
When he purred - she heard soft growling,
called him *Good Dog*.

They never spoke the same language.
Words changed with the odd missing letter -
was it *stay* or *stray*?

Like a Blessing

Published in The Frogmore Papers, #103, 2024 [23]

Do you remember when we climbed
to the top of the mountain before dawn,
the cold emptiness, the vast starry sky,
the steep track of hard stone under our feet,
and we watched the day materialising slowly,
a glow, a glimmer, then a diffusion of light
over us, and me with my mouth organ
bending the notes of 'Sun Arise' into the wind?

Do you remember how time ran through the air
painting the east in colours we could not believe
- blush-red, silver and yellow, orange, bright green -
the heavens alight, and above us the palest blue.
And hanging there, mid-air, the morning star
shining like a blessing - shining for us -
and when we turned and looked to the west
the sky was still dark, with pale stars lingering?

And do you remember how quickly the colour
drained away, and the last of the night and
the stars were gone, and the ecstasy when
the sun's rays touched us, bringing warmth,
and, chilled and hungry, we retraced our steps
down the shadowy slopes, and back at the camp
we lit the stove; ah, surely you remember
the smell of the bacon, and the hot coffee?

Tanager

Published in The Pierian, February 2024 [24]

I just had this recollection of the time I stood on your veranda
looking out between the plants that your green fingers had put
there; plants that always seemed to thrive.

And then, in the small fruit tree outside the garden, beyond the
gate, I saw a sayaca tanager,
a flash of gorgeous turquoise, teal and sapphire.

And I thought *what's such a dandy doing in a suburban street?*
Then it was gone; but the moment stayed, etched in my mind,
I associate it with you. Now you are gone too.

The Repair Shop
Published in Acumen #111, January 2025 [25]

Time moves in one direction, memory in another.
We are that strange species that constructs artefacts
... to counter the ... flow of forgetting. — William Gibson

Give me, please, this evening hour
of rest, let me sit safely here
to watch the show, alone at home,
in the quiet of this room,
my wife busy nearby, elsewhere,
as another day ends.

I have chosen this programme
from all those that tell of the past,
carefully put by for just such a time
when, worn down by the horrors
that trouble so many parts of the world,
I need peace for my mind.

Give me, please, this evening hour
of calm, to see as the stories unfold
once again, the love of decency,
kindness, skill, craft and care,
people fixing things from the past,
the undoing of damage and wear.

We cannot pretend inhumanity
ever will end - that's not the point.
Childhood innocence turns into doubt,
and doubt to despair, but still we go on.
We see, with soft eyes, the giving,
the healing, the hope, the repair.

Corvid

Published in London Grip, #54, Winter 2024 [26]

Rook, blackness manifest,
taking off from a shingle roof.
You are ur-crow, all crow,
pure essence of crow.

Rook from the first rook,
rising in ragged disorder,
blackness going your own way
night-in-day darkness.

Rook in flight, ghoul, spirit,
strange revenant, dark lord,
embodiment of indifference,
blackness become crow.

Pillar of Salt

Published in New Contexts: 6, 2024 [27]

When I turn the page, I see
the next poem is by someone
who has the same name as you,

who lives close to where you lived.
I find myself thinking about you
and how, by chance, we met.

That was half a lifetime ago,
but I wonder if you still remember
how special the moment seemed.

That first date we shared,
as if there was something in the air,
as if we'd always be together.

I read the poem. It's about choice,
about not looking back. About
making the best of what we have.

Constraint

Published in The Dawntreader, #68, Autumn 2024 [28]

Rain whispers in the city, a murmur
indicting the concrete, the roofs and the roads
which lie everywhere covering the earth.
Earth waits patiently.

Cars pass, as they must, for everyone
is going somewhere, urgently.
Tyres hiss in disapprobation.
Is the complainant the rain or the road?

Earth listens to the whispering,
languishing, waiting for justice.
It isn't the moment.
Its day will come.

Star Gazing - Together

Published in Dream Catcher #50, 2025 [29]

In the clear cold air and the black of the night
I pause to look at the shimmering sky,
a vast array of dark and bright,
a keening wind, an awesome sight,
the planet turns, the stars go by.

I sense my father by my side,
together we gaze on the paradigm,
father and son at a great divide
for he is gone but the heavens abide,
and I am here looking back in time.

Waymarks taught by father to son
- Cassiopeia, Orion, the Plough -
he stands and points to hither and yon,
telling the names that will ever go on,
and I remember quietly now.

Alone in the dark, at the end of the day
I pause to look at the black of the sky,
the stars are spread in a vast array,
a keening wind sweeps all away,
  we stand together, he and I;
                    he and I.

Perpetual Swift

Published in Obsessed with Pipework, #106, 2024 [30]

Look carefully, and still
you can't tell them apart.
No individual swift,
only the substance of swift,
anonymous dark outlines,
black-but-not-black, curved
steel in swinging flight.

Or swift by name and nature,
reckless, kinetic, a life force,
singularities of unknowability.
Swift-flying, now, yesterday,
last month, last year. And then
tomorrow traversing the world,
gone away, back next year.

Swift has always been swift,
is timeless and for certain.
Our fathers saw perpetual swift.
After us, swift will go on,
not this or that one, just swift,
pure motion ravelling the sky.
Swift, swifter, swiftest.

Concern

Published in South Poetry, #69, 2024 [31]

Concern
is like when you suddenly see white petals flutter
from the hawthorn blossom

(in a gentle breeze)

just a few days after standing exactly here
and feeling that urgent exhilaration
at the sight of the whole, radiant, sunlit hedgerow

(which made you want to thank *Whomsoever
There Is* waiting to have someone, maybe you,
notice how achingly beautiful life becomes
in fleeting moments, waiting to have someone,
maybe you, show gratitude at the thought that
the dispiriting days of long winter have gone,
that joy and fulness, and days of easy summer
stretch out before you)

but now reminded
that nothing can last forever, including you.

No Quarter

Published in Pennine Platform, #95, 2024 [32]

in memory of Marie Colvin (1956-2012)

America, much good has come from there,
much truth. Remember Marie Colvin,
foreign correspondent, went everywhere
- like Chechnya, reporting from within
a war zone, escaping through the mountains.
In East Timor - with troops threatening nearby
to kill women and children, she remained.
Sri Lanka cost her the sight of one eye.

Undeterred, elegant in her black patch,
she carried on throughout the Arab Spring,
getting her stories out, every dispatch
exposing human rights abuse, reporting
the facts, careless of bullets or bombs.
Her last conflict, Syria; killed in Homs.

Psaltery

Published in The Cannon's Mouth, # 91, 2024 [33]

for Begoña Olavide

Your music runs in my head, springing
  from fingers, strings, a box, a lap,
    your art holding us together
      out of the flow of time and place.

I delve into the meaning of words:
  psalm is a hymn, a plaintive liturgy,
    psalter, a book of psalms,
      psaltery, a spirit-house of sound,

and your words are chimera
  of mind, voice and glyph
    taking us back to bone, wood and stone;
      dark turns to light, and I am home.

Left Hanging

Published in The Cannon's Mouth, # 91, 2024 [34]

The Suicide Act 1961

When I was small, our neighbour
was old Mr. Hall. Between us
a fence. Mother said he was widowed
- a word that to me made no sense.

Kind Mr. Hall passed me sweets
over the fence, and he took me to see
his greenhouse: tomato plants,
an odd earthy smell, heat and humidity.

One day an ambulance stopped
in the street, two dutiful men with
a stretcher, and then, under a blanket,
an indistinct shape and two bare feet.

A crime in a greenhouse, forgotten,
until, from the vine, once again
that odd earthy smell - a blanket,
bare feet, and two ambulance men.

So long ago! He was a lonely old man,
the sun still shone, but no more
sweets passed over the fence.
I was a child and he - he was gone.

Samantha

Published in Lighten Up Online (LUPO) #67, 2024 [35]

Samantha was a teacher at a local primary school,
she was young and keen and pretty, and unquestionably cool.
She hadn't long been qualified, she didn't earn a lot,
so she needed to be careful with the little that she got.

Samantha loved her job, she believed it well worth while
and she always maintained discipline, with tolerance and guile.
The kids were never easy though, in fact a few were tough
and the worst of them was Johnnie, a challenge sure enough.

Johnnie was a lively boy but, if we're being blunt,
he was disruptive, so Samantha made him sit right at the front.
And there, since he found himself right under teacher's gaze,
he decided, if he could do, to amend his wayward ways.

Each day when it was lunchtime Samantha used to eat
at Luigi's transport café, *The Vesuvius Retreat.*
The food was cheap and cheerful but Samantha always knew
that the *Special of the Day* would be good, and tasty too.

One day the lunchtime special on the menu was *couscous,*
traditional from Morocco, billed as *très délicieux.*
So Samantha thought she might as well as give couscous a try;
it came with egg and lettuce, but she found it rather dry.

That very afternoon, as it happened, was the one
that *Ofsted* chose to visit - of warnings there were none!
Miss Jones, the Head, decided that the lesson they'd inspect
was Samantha's, and Samantha was unable to object.

She was teaching well, as usual, but didn't know, alas,
that couscous has a tendency to make a lot of gas.
The aching in her tummy kept increasing as she taught
and she found that her predicament was fast becoming fraught.

Samantha did her best to conceal her agitation
but the couscous kept fermenting - and she felt a desperation
to relieve the awful pressure that was tearing her apart,
until, you guessed, she blew it in a cataclysmic fart!

You'd have to use the Richter scale to calibrate the blast.
Consternation followed, the inspectors were aghast.
Samantha could have died, it was so humiliating,
she knew that there'd be trouble - oh, it was devastating.

But though she was despairing, in her awful hour of need
Samantha thought to lay the blame on Johnnie for the deed.
She shouted *Stop that, Johnnie!* and Johnnie shouted *Whoa!*
Certainly I'll stop it Miss — which way did it go?

There is no happy ending to this sad and sorry tale.
Ofsted ruled the school as *Inadequate* or *Fail*,
and Samantha was dismissed because the *Special of the Day*
from *Vesuvius* erupted, and blew her clean away.

What The Thunder Said

Published in Lighten Up Online (LUPO), #66, 2024 [36]

('What The Thunder Said' is an online poetry-information group)

Last week I clicked a Facebook link - in quest of things poetic,
to my surprise, instead I got the female form aesthetic.
The image showed in detail all the bits one should not see,
she was lying there exposed and I thought *goodness gracious
me!*

I was shocked by what I saw in her lack of inhibition.
It was not, it seemed, an advert for a poetry competition,
or the cover of a book for a poet's new collection,
and I wondered if I should, or shouldn't, make a close
inspection.

I know that art is various, you'll not find me neglecting
those views I'm not enamoured of but maybe need respecting,
and though one man's erotica is someone else's vice,
I thought the titillation there fell somewhat short of *nice*.

So I clicked the little icon and requested the removal
of the image as unseemly, and unfit for the approval
of poets of all persuasions, including the depraved,
and resisted the temptation of a screenshot, swiftly saved.

Quite soon, I got a message from the Facebook censor corps
to thank me for reporting the pornography I saw.
It's now been taken down, they said, and I thought *Given time,
that wanton naked Venus might provoke a bit of rhyme.*

The Road Taken

Published in Light, an American webzine, Winter 2024 [37]

after Robert Frost

Two roads diverged in a yellow wood,
and knowing I could not travel both
and still be honest, long I stood
and looked down one, the road for good,
to where it bent in the undergrowth;

then took the other; I didn't care,
for me it had the better claim,
a road for a man with *savoir-faire*
intent on making money somewhere,
and I am a man who knows no shame.

A fool would have chosen the other way
and ended up in a wooden shack.
Oh, I wanted a mansion and playboy pay
and if every dog will have its day
I planned to stay ahead of the pack.

I shall be rich till the day I die
somewhere ages and ages hence:
two roads diverged in a wood, and I,
I wanted much more than to just get by,
and that has made all the difference.

Painting the Fence

Published in The Lake, July 2024 [38]

Three of us for each one then,
though they are mostly gone and you are old.
You're busy painting the fence
to make it last a few more years.
You know that everyone wants more
than ever you had - that's human nature,

well, nature's what we say. You start
another board, doing the long edge first;
the only nature you can see
is when you look up -
two rattling magpies, a red kite spiralling by,
and hurtling swifts - the dodgems of the skies.

You plumped for Medium Oak;
you stretch and reach, knees bend.
You know that Earth's resilient, but it can't keep up -
three now for each one then.
What will happen? Life goes on,
it must, it always does - and everyone

wants to consume: neater, faster, smarter.
You do - we all do. How will it end?
The boards are cheapo knotty pine with holes -
go on, peep through, you see
your neighbour's washing on the line.
And suddenly you're back, a kid again

seeing Her-Next-Door's astounding lacy bras
and skimpy pants;
of course, by now she's gone -
popped her clogs, moved on - gone to dust.
Medium Oak tarting up cheap pine,
it's looking good - the fence - appearances,

pretence - isn't that what Life's about?
But it's no use us pretending Earth
can cope with three-times then - and rising still.
The birds don't worry though,
they're going on, surviving, those that can,
in spite of man. Going, going, gone.

Today I Fell Off an Ostrich

Published in Light, an American webzine, Winter 2024 [39]

Today I fell off an ostrich
and I feel quite remarkably glad.
It's a thing to recall when there's nothing at all
so opportunistically mad.

You may say to fall off an ostrich
is something you'd rather not try
and in any case where would you find one to spare,
and how would you mount it, and why?

But today, I fell off an ostrich,
just look at the bruises - and yet,
when every abrasion has gone, the occasion
is one I shall never forget.

Yes, I actually fell off an ostrich;
the locals looked on in delight
with joy unconfined. Me on my behind
in the dust and the dirt, what a sight!

You may say that to fall off an ostrich
is in fact merely par for the course
but think, how absurd to fall off a bird
instead of a bike or a horse!

Doggerland

Published in Impspired, #30, 2024 [40]

We are rushing along over a lost land,
hastening towards our destination.
If the gods of earth, sea and air allow,
we shall arrive tomorrow morning.

No-one looks down. Why should we?
There is only black water to be seen.
But someone knows what's there,
in the eye of the mind, time gone.

We are on cruise control. The sun
is starting to set. We maintain
an exact altitude. Below, mammoths
in groups roam, unseen, unseeing.

They do not look up as we pass.
Why should they? We are not here.
It is green, it is summer, the animals
wander at will, there is plenty.

Passing, they mark the landscape.
Soon they will leave their corpses;
when we come we shall find them
and marvel. We do not come yet.

In the Park of My Mind

Published in Impspired, #30, 2024 [41]

Goiânia, Brazil

We went, granddaughter and I,
on a slow afternoon, to the park.
Not much of a park, perhaps,
but somewhere to go.

Two steel seesaws, and two
small swings, we tried them all,
fun, of a kind, on a slow afternoon,
for a girl and a man.

One swing creaked, just the one.
Why?, she wanted to know.
Because it needs oiling, I said,
we can oil it tomorrow.

We never went back.
I'm still here but she's gone,
and in the park of my mind
the creak of the swing goes on.

Dog Days

Published in Impspired, #30, 2024 [42]

July is such a nothing month. We know
that July days still are long and bright,
but the equinox has gone and although
the sun sets late there's a change of light.

And as the day's length wanes, plants in flow
sensing that things are on the turn,
hesitate, the sap pauses, starts to go
into reverse. Green leaves begin to burn

to yellow, brown and gold. Farmers prepare
for the frantic harvest rush. Holidays
from school, people get away to anywhere,
the silly season, the doldrums, dog days.

In July, summer's suddenly on hold.
Uneasy hints of coming dark and cold.

Oblivion
Published in London Grip, September 2024 [43]

The fact that Stalin's despotic rule
resulted in the death of between 3.3 million
and 7.5 million people in Ukraine,
and 1 to 2 million people in Kazakhstan,
or 14 million people across the Soviet Union,

and the fact that I was made explicitly aware
of this rather more than fifty years ago,
but had forgotten completely and managed,
somehow, to go quite happily on
with my life, until reminded of it just now,

probably provides more insight into
the mysterious dark matter, that makes up
about 85% of everything in the universe,
than achieved so far by theoretical physicists.

I want you to close your eyes and imagine

Published in London Grip, September 2024 [44]

You are here with friends sharing your poems.
Suddenly, there's an explosion, and you know,
from the direction and an inexplicable instinct,
that this time it's *your* home that has been hit.

You shout out *No! No! No!* and set off running,
your friends run after you. Yes! it was your home!
Look at the dust rising! Neighbours are there,
and you can see straight into your living room,

smashed furniture, the TV, the pictures, water
gushing from the broken pipes of your bathroom.
There's no sign of your wife, or of your children.
Oh! God in Heaven, you cry, *save them!*

But they tell you *She's dead, your wife is dead!*
And they can't find your daughter. Your son,
he's alive but injured, they're caring for him.
It's all a nightmare of grief and rubble.

What will you do? Where will you start?
She cannot be dead - it's not possible,
and where *is* your daughter? You call her name
again and again, *Oh my daughter, my girl!*

Your son, now in your arms, stunned, hurt,
but alive, breathing! You hold him close.
Where *is* your daughter? You fear the worst.
Now open your eyes and remember.

It really happened

Section Two: Translations of Poems into English from Portuguese and Spanish - Six poems

Early in 2014 I was persuaded by a friend to attempt the translation of 15 poems from Spanish into English, to be included in the cover notes of an album of Spanish poems set to music (see Endnote [33] for *Psaltery*). I had never before translated a poem, so it was quite a challenge. In due course the album appeared and can be found on the internet under the title *De Un Tiempo a Esta Parte*.

In 2017 I wrote an article with the title *Poetry in Translation* for *The Blue Nib* [45], in which I described the often quite formidable challenges one faces in attempting to achieve the successful representation of a poem written in one language in a different language.

Some people maintain that translating poems is actually impossible.[46] Among the obvious difficulties are maintaining form, rhyme-pattern (if there are rhymes), rhythm and mood between the two languages. Then there are differences in vocabulary, idiom, and allusion to deal with. However, without translation we would not have access to vast amounts of world poetry, for example, *Beowulf,* the *Divine Comedy,* the *Rubaiyat of Omar Khayyam,* or, indeed, to any foreign language poetry.

So far, I have translated more than 40 poems into English, mostly from Spanish, but also Portuguese, languages I know quite well, The originals were written from as far back as the twelfth century up to the present day and, of course, one must try to represent each poem in a way appropriate to the time and language in which it was first written.

In the following pages are six of my translations that have been published, and I am including the originals alongside my English versions. That will enable readers to see the compromises I made to try to achieve the best possible results. Sometimes one has to modify the rhyme scheme or even change a basic idea in an effort to present a poem in English that could stand as a *good* poem in its own right.

I do, in fact, feel quite strongly that the originals of translated poems should always be made available. Readers may have at least a little knowledge of the source language so it allows comparisons and scrutiny of what the translator has done. I have seen some awful translations in print. An egregious example is the translation of the title of one of Jorge Luis Borges' poems *El Enemigo Generoso* as *The Generous Friend* when it should, in fact, be *The Generous Enemy.* [47]

In 2021, as part of the Stamford Verse Festival of that year, I gave a sell-out presentation on *Iberian & Latin-American Poetry* in the Gallery at the town's Arts Centre. It included 14 of my translations of poems by poets from Spain, Portugal, Brazil, Argentina, Chile, Peru, Mexico and Cuba. The ability to read, understand, appreciate, translate and finally share wonderful poems from other languages and cultural traditions is, I feel, a great privilege and I hope you will enjoy reading and thinking about the six translations that follow.

Twin Souls - Emilia Pardo Bazán

Published in Orbis, #179, 2017 [48]

Two halves of one dewdrop
and the sea taking it
deep to its cold breast unlocks
one pearl, embracing it;

atoms of rose fragrance
that the wind, coaxing, combines;
notes in a harp's cadence
of equal time;

twin stars of a single birth
sharing one orbit;
twin souls that on this sad earth
one mind inhabit;

lovers are doubtless like this
sharing one faith,
and perhaps, beyond the abyss,
love in another place.

Almas Gemelas
Emilia Pardo Bazán (1851-1921)

Mitades de una gota de rocío
con que el mar, al beberla,
en lo profundo de su seno frío
cuaja una sola perla;

átomos del perfume de la rosa
que el viento mece unido;
notas que vibra el arpa melodiosa
iguales en sonido;

estrellas dobles que en el alto cielo
una órbita describen;
almas gemelas que en el triste suelo
de un pensamiento viven;

esto sin duda son los que se quieren
su fe guardando entera,
y acaso pasarán cuando aquí mueran
a amarse en otra esfera.

My Town - Cora Coralina

Published in Orbis, #178, 2016 [49]

Goiás, my town…
I am that lover
of your short,
narrow streets,
your indecisive
streets that come
and go,
one with another.
I am the plain little girl of the Lapa bridge.
I am Ana.

I am that woman
who has grown old,
forgotten;
in your squares and your sombre alleyways
I tell stories
and foresee what will be.
I sing your past,
I sing your future.

I live in your churches
and fine houses
and red-tiled roofs
and walls.

I am that old wall
green with ferns
where the crooked jasmine tree
leans,
fragrant
in the dingy alleyway.

I am those houses
that conspire
whispering one to another.   [continues →

Minha Cidade

Cora Coralina (1889-1985)

Goiás, minha cidade...
Eu sou aquela amorosa
de tuas ruas estreitas,
curtas,
indecisas,
entrando,
saindo
uma das outras.
Eu sou aquela menina feia da ponte da Lapa.
Eu sou Aninha.

Eu sou aquela mulher
que ficou velha,
esquecida,
nos teus larguinhos e nos teus becos tristes,
contando estórias,
fazendo adivinhação.
Cantando teu passado.
Cantando teu futuro.

Eu vivo nas tuas igrejas
e sobrados
e telhados
e paredes.

Eu sou aquele teu velho muro
verde de avencas
onde se debruça
um antigo jasmineiro,
cheiroso
na ruinha pobre e suja.

Eu sou estas casas
encostadas
cochichando umas com as outras.

[continues →

I am the branches of those trees
whose names no-one knows
and no-one loves,
that have neither flowers nor fruits,
but that give shade to the weary
and shelter to the birds.

I am the stems
of the weeds
that spring from cracks in the stones.
Tough.
Obstinate.
Indomitable.
Attacked.
Ill-treated.
Down-trodden.
And reborn.

I am the resistance of your hills,
rugged,
lush with flowers,
torn by axes,
lashed and lacerated.
Burned by fire.
Overgrazed.
Destroyed
and renewed.
My life,
my feelings,
my sense of beauty,
all the tremblings
of my sensibilities as a woman,
are rooted here.

I am the plain little girl
of the Lapa bridge.
I am Ana.

Eu sou a ramada
dessas árvores,
sem nome e sem valia,
sem flores e sem frutos,
de que gostam
a gente cansada e os pássaros vadios.

Eu sou o caule
dessas trepadeiras sem classe,
nascidas na frincha das pedras:
Bravias.
Renitentes.
Indomáveis.
Cortadas.
Maltratadas.
Pisadas.
E renascendo.

Eu sou a dureza desses morros,
revestidos,
enflorados,
lascados a machado,
lanhados, lacerados.
Queimados pelo fogo.
Pastados.
Calcinados
e renascidos.
Minha vida,
meus sentidos,
minha estética,
todas as virações
de minha sensibilidade de mulher,
têm, aqui, suas raízes.

Eu sou a menina feia
da ponte da Lapa.
Eu sou Aninha.

Galleries - Antonio Machado
Published in The Blue Nib, #20, 2018 [50]

I have seen my soul in dreams...
In the ethereal space
where worlds turn,
a mad star, a swift
comet with its red
hair on fire ...

I have seen my soul in dreams,
like a silvery river
of gentle rippling waves
that flow quietly...

I have seen my soul in dreams,
like a long, narrow
shadowy passageway,
lit up at the end...

Perhaps my soul has
the laughing light of the fields,
and its fragrances reach
from there, from the bright depth...

I have seen my soul in dreams...
It was an empty space
and a dry broken tree
near the white path.

Galerías
Antonio Machado (1875-1939)

Yo he visto mi alma en sueños...
En el etéreo espacio
donde los mundos giran,
un astro loco, un raudo
cometa con los rojos
cabellos incendiados...

Yo he visto mi alma en sueños
cual río plateado,
de rizas ondas lentas
que fluyen dormitando...

Yo he visto mi alma en sueños
como un estrecho y largo
corredor tenebroso,
de fondo iluminado...

Acaso mi alma tenga
risueña luz de campo,
y sus aromas lleguen
de allá, del fondo claro...

Yo he visto mi alma en sueños...
Era un desierto llano
y un árbol seco y roto
hacia el camino blanco.

from The Eternal Ray - Miguel Hernández
Published in Orbis, #205, 2023 [51]

I confess to a tenderness for your accent,
 I admit to a neediness for your company.
 I acknowledge an illness of melancholy
and a restlessness for the air you frequent.

Emptiness is what I feel in my torment,
 anxiousness for your elegant beauty,
 your forgiveness, your consoling sympathy,
your kindliness for my wounded intent.

Oh, tenderness, neediness and illness!
 Your sustaining kisses, my contentment.
 I miss them in spring; I die each May.

I want you, my flower of loneliness,
 to soothe my mind and, refulgent,
 to shine on me your eternal ray.

de El Rayo Que No Cesa
Miguel Hernández (1910-1942)

Una querencia tengo por tu acento,
 una apetencia por tu compañía
 y una dolencia de melancolía
por la ausencia del aire de tu viento.

Paciencia necesita mi tormento,
 urgencia de tu garza galanía,
 tu clemencia solar mi helado día,
tu asistencia la herida en que lo cuento.

¡Ay querencia, dolencia y apetencia!:
 tus sustanciales besos, mi sustento,
 me faltan y me muero sobre mayo.

Quiero que vengas, flor desde tu ausencia,
 a serenar la sien del pensamiento
 que desahoga en mí su eterno rayo.

Even a Tree - Javier Bergia

Javier Bergia
Published in Dream Catcher, #48, 2024 [52]

I travel along through the beautiful days of the life that I live
marked, as I am, by the loves I have had that I loved to the
last.
Pleasures, adventures, and caring more tender than any
should give,
years full of music, happy, impulsive, wherever I passed.

How short the adventure, inviting, exciting - the journey I'm on.
Why should I leave when I only want more and I'm having
such fun?
This lingering kiss, oh! hard as it is, uncertain or worse,
will come to an end and shadows descend, unfeeling, perverse.

Time is a tango, a frenzied fandango in crimsons and blues.
We take it for granted, until, disenchanted, we falter and lose.
Our memories go, we forget what we know, and, beyond or
above,
the end of the story, a transient glory; I die for your love.

But even a tree, that lives longer than me, must wither and burn
and, scattered the embers that no one remembers, will never
return.

Palito de Madera

Caminare despacio por los hermosos días que me toco vivir,
que llenos de arañazos que dejan los amores que sin querer perdí;
colmaron de ventura, cariño y más ternura de la que pueda
uno pedir,
los años tan dichosos de música y antojos; allá por donde fui.

Que corto este viaje, que rabia y que coraje, que ganas de seguir.
Porque habré de marcharme, queriendo pues quedarme,
quisiera repetir.
Que lánguido este beso tan duro como un hueso, incierto y tan hostil.
Será que hay que dar paso, no hay vida sin ocaso, nostálgico
y febril.

El tiempo es como un tango, frenético y fandango, celeste y carmesí.
Se vive acostumbrado, mas luego despojado se muere porque si.
Se pierde la memoria, no queda ni la gloria, si acaso algún
rumor.
Que insólito fracaso, sentir que ya de paso, me muero por tu amor.

Qué pena de arbolito, que verde y tan bonito, tenerse que partir.
Palito de madera, ceniza de una hoguera que se ha de
consumir.

Who would leave - Miguel de Cervantes

Published in Acumen, #109, 2024 [53]

Who would leave the green and fragrant pasture
  with its refreshing plants and cooling streams?
Who exert himself in chasing after
  the agile hare or fierce wild boar's esteems?

Who, loving its calls and for its sweet voice pining,
  would not keep a singing bird displayed?
Who, on long, hot afternoons reclining
  would scorn to seek the pleasant woodland shade?

Who would choose to seek, in mindless fashion
  and fear of jealousy, rage, anger, pain,
    the love that proving false destroys mankind?

The countryside is where I find my passion,
  it's rose and jasmine that my heart enchain,
    born free, it is by freedom I'm defined.

Quién dejará, del Verde Prado Umbroso
Miguel de Cervantes (1548-1616)

¿Quién dejará, del verde prado umbroso,
  las frescas yerbas y las frescas fuentes?
  ¿Quién, de seguir con pasos diligentes
la suelta liebre o jabalí cerdoso?

¿Quién, con el son amigo y sonoroso,
  no detendrá las aves inocentes?
  ¿Quién, en las horas de la siesta, ardientes,
no buscará en las selvas el reposo,

por seguir los incendios, los temores,
  los celos, iras, rabias, muertes, penas
    del falso amor que tanto aflige al mundo?

Del campo son y han sido mis amores,
  rosas son y jazmines mis cadenas,
    libre nací, y en libertad me fundo.

Afterword

In my experience, it isn't easy to get poems accepted for publication by poetry editors, and I've gone into the difficulties, and suggested strategies and tactics, in my previous collections, *As Red as Rubies* and *Schrödinger's Eco-Cat.* I will not, therefore, repeat that here, except to say that it's a hit-and-miss process. Quite a few of my poems that I'd very much like to have accepted have not found a home, but I like to think that some of them might still do so. [54]

My outlook on life, as represented in my poetry, is informed by secularism and humanism, which I consider offer far better guides to morality than those incidental to religions with their conflicting doctrines and irrational beliefs. The fact that the main political parties in the UK think fit to promote the management and administration of schools by religious organisations, and so permit the access of authoritarian faith figures to children, especially primary school children whose minds are not yet mature, will one day be correctly understood, I believe, as state-sponsored child abuse.

Although *religion* has had me writing enough poems to practically fill another book, editors seem unwilling to publish such work. The sole exception in *Blades of Grass* is, perhaps, *Darwin*, which is why I wonder if the editor actually noticed that it is a religious satire.

Similarly, editors seem generally reluctant to accept poems about intimate love (surely love's deepest expression). Edward Hirsch (Endnote [16]) says *There are few things more discomfiting to hardened critical readers than a poem of naked and unembarrassed desire.* In this collection perhaps *Waiting Area* might be classed as of the genre, and I sent it to a number of editors, some of whom were complimentary about it, before Ian Gouge of *New Contexts* finally published it. I have written what I think are better and more direct poems about erotic love which are, so far, unpublished.

In the end, though, I think those of us who enjoy trying to make poems are writing primarily for ourselves. However I am immensely grateful to the hard-working editors who have accepted those of my own efforts. I would encourage all who are motivated to express themselves in verse to share their work with others in open-mic poetry meetings and online. But I also suggest you find and read a few contemporary poetry magazines and anthologies, and then submit your work for possible publication. It is a fine feeling of validation when one of what you regard as your precious poems finds its editor.

Acknowledgements

I'd like to thank Stamford Arts Centre, and in particular Karen Burrows, the Events Administrator, for her steadfast dedication to encouraging and promoting poetry in the South Lincolnshire area over the years.

The circumstances in which this collection has appeared changed when Steve Cawte, the founding editor of 'Impspired', who agreed to promote its publication and its aim of raising funds for Papworth Hospital, passed away during the course of its preparation. But I am very grateful to the remarkable Nikki and Charlie Cawte for their continuing support.

Finally, thanks to family and friends, and to all who have given your time to reading my poems.

Endnotes

[1] I am besotted by swifts and always look out for their arrival and departure. I had last seen swifts on August 14th, over my garden, so to see *'a last, lone swift'* on August 21st, the evening Steve died, was remarkable. The poem was accepted for publication by Charlie Cawte, Steve's son, who has taken over editorship at *'Impspired'*. It appeared in Charlie's first, special, edition of just 30 poems in February, published in memory of Steve, with support by Mary Farrell.

[2] In these days when there is so much mention of *mental health issues*, I'd like to say how much peace of mind I invariably experience from gazing up into the blue of the sky and observing the clouds that are constantly moving and changing. If there are any birds there, that is a bonus. A few years ago I bought myself a copy of *The Cloud Book* (produced in association with the Met Office), and when my friend John Graydon retired, with the prospect of working in his wonderful garden, I gave him a copy of the book to help him appreciate the beauty of the skies. I recently gave another copy to a very elderly friend (and distant relative) who, though confined to three rooms in his home, is able to see a blessed patch of sky out of one of his windows. It reminds me of the lines from Oscar Wilde's *The Ballad of Reading Gaol*:

I never saw a man who looked / With such a wistful eye / Upon that little tent of blue / Which prisoners call the sky...

[3] The title poem of *Schrödinger's Eco-Cat* attempts to raise public awareness of how even the slightest human actions inevitably affect the environment; there are now more than 8,000 million people on earth, perhaps more than our planet can sustain. The best hope for humanity of finding solutions to the problems of over-exploitation of natural resources is through technology, but if politicians fail to provide an appropriate legal framework then, I fear, the situation will become impossible. My concern is more for future generations than my own, for example that of my grandchildren. We need to pay for the impact each one of us causes, and the best way to calculate *how much* we should each pay is via carbon taxes, so that those who make the greatest impact pay the most. That is what I try to say in this poem. The Seventh Quarry is a print magazine based in Swansea.

4 Samuel Johnson was no fool, in fact he was extremely erudite. The *Oxford Dictionary of National Biography* calls him *arguably the most distinguished man of letters in English history*. Yet his ideas about where swallows go when they disappear from our view in autumn now invite the kind of absurd response that *Swallow Tale* attempts. I love that science makes so much progress that the past can seem ridiculous. So many superstitions demolished - and yet so many still remain...

5 It *was* springtime, but it *wasn't* Harrington Street. It was actually Stanley Street, but I needed a name with three syllables. That's what we call poetic license. This poem could, I think, have been written *only* by an earth scientist and it is a good romp through Earth History. I like the fact that everything narrated is pretty-much accurate. In form, it's a ballad, and I hope readers will enjoy the rollocking rhythm and rhyme.

6 I wrote two poems about the coal that washes up on the beaches of Northumberland, this and *Sea Coal*, which was published in *The Cannon's Mouth* and appeared in *As Red as Rubies*. I think that my sensibilities as an earth scientist were fundamental to both.

7 *Night Flight* was written during Covid lockdown, a surreal time even to those of us who went through it, but in the published version of the poem I removed the specific references to that event. I like the poem for its contrast of the impassivity of wild animals with the concern of humanity about situations that threaten our wellbeing. In that sense, the poem is of continuing relevance. Not much in the world moves me as much as witnessing sudden spectacles of nature in all their detachment.

8 *Quarry (disused)* draws, again, on my geological background. It is written, in my imagination, about the beautiful town of Stamford, designated, in 1967, as England's first urban conservation area. All towns built of local stone come from local quarries and just as the towns bustle, so the quarries often lie empty and abandoned. The irony is that stone from the quarries often marks the graves of those who lived in the towns that came from the quarries. I like the close word-play of the poem.

⁹ This short poem (in form a triolet using dactylic beats) records an event one winter several years before it was written when my mother and I were observing the white wilderness of snow across from my home, and out of nowhere a carrion crow suddenly appeared. Another moment of unexpected witnessing of nature.

¹⁰ This became the title poem for the collection. I was walking my daughter's much-loved dog, Rio, a cross between a German Shepherd and a Collie (see the book's cover), a handsome chap and a carefree family pet, along the course of the Roman Carr Dyke near Bourne. One of the poem's influences was the twelve years I spent researching, recording and writing-up my family history, but a heightened awareness of earth history - and therefore 'earth' as in 'soil', is surely there too. Also, note those 'unending chains' of *Springtime on Harrington Street* again.

¹¹ For six years I volunteered at Westfield, a local primary school, helping Year 5 children with their reading on a one-to-one basis. It was wonderful being with the youngsters, doing something I felt was so fundamental to life. Another ballad.

¹² A bit like *Quarry (disused),* this poem builds on an imaginary mountain, perhaps from the Lake District or western Scotland, personifying it as a living thing. There is certainly an ecological awareness, as befits the times we live in. The sycamore trees and the sheep of the farms hark back to those I was once familiar with in the Pennine uplands of Lancashire and Yorkshire.

¹³ *Loss in Old Age* is a poem of hope made out of grief. There is, I think, an incredible fortitude, not often-enough recognised, in many elderly people, and several individuals come readily to my mind. A copy of the poem was taken by one such courageous person and passed around among her octogenarian friends. She was kind enough to tell me it was much appreciated.

¹⁴ There is an obvious resonance between this and the previous poem. It appeared in the *Friends* issue of *The Alchemy Spoon,* under the title *Brother-in-law* and relates to the loss of the oldest of my three Brazilian brothers-in-law, in November 2018. Nowadays we would probably say he suffered from significant mental-health problems, for which he received no help. He was clever but poorly educated, and he caused his parents, his wife and his children many moments of sadness and sometimes despair. But I liked him.

[15] This is a surreal poem - ludic, one might say - about the black vultures that are so common in and over Brazilian cities; they also feature in *Ellipsis* (in *Schrödinger's Eco-Cat*). They are about as ugly a bird as you will ever see, but fly magnificently and do a great job of disposing of offal and other noxious waste. These particular vultures live in Goiânia.

[16] Service of my Honda Jazz in Peterborough. At the time, the book I was reading was, I believe, Edward Hirsch's wonderful *How to Read a Poem and Fall in Love with Poetry*. But though I have searched more than once, I have never since found the quote about *the early marriage bed*. Maybe one day...

[17] Another poem with an element of the surreal. I was travelling, alone, through the fissile shale mountains of the Southern Uplands of Scotland listening to an enthralling BBC Radio programme about the life of Picasso. The night was black, it was very late and the road was empty; the miles slipped away.

[18] Various, perhaps unrelated, elements come together in this poem. A big blonde man with a lawnmower who might, or might not, have been a former soldier, a definite former soldier I once worked with who clearly had PTSD difficulties after seeing active service in the Falkland Islands, and the Cenotaph in Bourne on Remembrance Day. The reference to Terry Street is from Douglas Dunn's fine poem *A Removal from Terry Street*.

[19] *In Transit* tells of when my wife travelled, in August 1982, from Holland to Brazil via Morocco. She had with her our daughters, Rebecca who was then 2 years 4 months old, and Elise who was a baby of just five months. They had to stay overnight in a hotel near the airport and on the following day were treated abominably while waiting hours for their *Air Morocco* connecting flight.

[20] It's always pleasing to have a more lighthearted poem accepted for publication. In this one, earth history, my liking of Richard Dawkins' writing and my familiarity with the Bible come together. I'm not convinced that the editor of LUPO actually spotted the religious satire that drives the poem. It is aimed mainly at the American Evangelicals who support Donald Trump; they scare me.

[21] Sometimes two poems emerge from the same initial insight, and it may be that both of them end up being accepted for publication. This has happened to me twice, once in relation to *sea coal*, a second time in relation to my Viking and his lawnmower; see note [18], above.

[22] This is an allegory, which, to me, is clear. But I'm not going to provide any clues. I have a suspicion that the *Strix* editors didn't really get it, but its weirdness appealed to them. And sometimes thats how poems are. On a (much) larger scale, think *Jabberwocky*.

[23] This is among my favourite poems. It goes back to a spring day in, probably, 1965 when my friend Steve Walthall and I camped on the northwestern slopes of Pendle Hill, above Clitheroe, and then climbed to its summit to watch the sun rise. It is, essentially, an account of what really happened and has always stayed with me. Steve and I did much hiking and camping together, including walking the Pennine Way from north to south in 12 days, and our two Duke of Edinburgh's Gold Award expeditions in the Lake District.

[24] The 'you' of this short poem was my Brazilian mother in law, Terezinha Pereira da Silva (1938-2013). She was a remarkable woman from a very difficult background who, among other talents (especially sewing and dressmaking), had the greenest of green fingers. I'm pleased that she was able to visit us in England, Portugal and Chile. *The Pierian* is an American webzine and magazine.

[25] The version of this poem accepted by *Acumen* comprises essentially the first three stanzas shown here. *The Repair Shop* is a programme from BBC Television.

[26] This poem also came out of *The Repair Shop* - a vignette when the camera showed a rook suddenly taking off from the top of one of the complex of buildings in which the programme is based. But the members of the crow family have always fascinated me. See, e.g. *'Crow Triolet'* on page 16.

27 *Pillar of Salt* came out of reading someone else's poem in one of the many poetry journals I have subscribed to over the years. Poems often include mention of where each poet lives and one particular poem got me imagining how things might have been if P, the poet, had married R, the reader when they met in their youth, instead of S who they actually did marry. And was P thinking of R in writing the poem? How cool would that have been? The title comes from one of the well-known bible stories which are so beautifully told, especially in *The King James* version.

28 I am always slightly surprised by the fact that land exists in perpetuity. The land we bury under construction will, one day, one way or another, reclaim itself. What is even *one* million years to land? The land outside my window as I write is about 200 million years old. *Its day will come.*

29 The original title was 'Star Gazing'. The poem is, broadly, a factual account of a time of special memories.

30 I am obsessed with swifts. I have written several poems about them but this is the first I have been lucky enough to see published. Swifts seem so entirely alien, so aloof, so individually unknowable - as if merely a commodity. They spend only about 12 weeks with us, breeding and raising their young, then undertake a 5,500 mile trip to the Congo basin where they spend the rest of the year. How mind-blowingly astonishing is that? See also *'Saying Goodbye'* on page 3.

31 This is another (rare) example of a poem that almost wrote itself in just a few minutes. Another example of Nature suddenly giving me a moment.

32 When I heard of Marie Colvin, and then researched her life online, I felt humbled to know that such an outstanding person, woman, reporter, had existed. The poem, of sonnet form, came out of that. Let's recognise the goodness in humanity - it doesn't often make the headlines...

[33] Begoña Olavide and her fellow musician Javier Bergia (see my translation *Even a Tree* on page 67) are Spanish artists who I have known for more than ten years, and was able to accompany when they performed at a Catherine of Aragon festival in Peterborough cathedral in 2018. I had previously translated the Spanish poems which they set to music and released on the CD *De Un Tiempo a Esta Parte*. Begoña is a virtuoso performer on the Spanish psaltery, using a beautiful instrument made by her husband, Carlos Paniagua. *Psaltery* is a poem I wrote after accompanying Begoña and Javier to a wonderful gig in Stamford Corn Exchange on the evening following their performance in the cathedral.

[34] Abolishing the crime of suicide was another significant step on the road to a more tolerant, more secular, society. This is a simple poem, but one that notices how abiding memories can be triggered by the senses, and the bafflement that children often feel when first confronted by the proximity of death.

[35] *Samantha* never existed, but the story of couscous creating a *lot of gas* did. It derived from the time I was working at Lídice in Brazil in 1975.

[36] This (lighthearted) poem recounts real circumstances, which the Muse insisted I versify. Nice that it got past Jerome Betts, the editor of LUPO.

[37] *Light* is an American poetry webzine that was pleased to take this parody of the American poet Robert Frost's much-loved poem *The Road Not Taken*.

[38] In my lifetime the world's population has risen from about 2.4 billion to over 8 billion, a factor of more than 3. I find this astounding and the implications are, I think, widely underestimated. The rapid and unpredictable changes in the Earth's atmosphere, hydrosphere and biosphere that humankind is causing by our demands to consume (or buy and discard) vast amounts of 'stuff' are, I fear, disrupting the ability of the planet to sustain human wellbeing. I explained my views further in the Afterword to Schrödinger's Eco-Cat. The poem is a soliloquy.

39 I wrote the original version of this poem early in 1973 following a visit to one of the world's earliest ostrich farms, at Oudtshoorn in South Africa. After watching a demonstration by local 'jockeys' I accepted the challenge of having a go myself (I was 27). I started off well, then suddenly found myself in the dirt, as described. A fellow visitor later told me that someone had grabbed one of the bird's feet to make it stumble and so throw me off. I wrote the poem very soon after, but revised it and submitted it to *Light* .

40 In August 2018 my wife and I, together with my sister and her partner, sailed from Southampton for a cruise to visit countries around the Baltic Sea. While traversing the North Sea, towards nightfall, I gazed at the black waters below me and saw, in my mind's eye, the former land area, exposed at the last glacial advance some 20,000 years ago, which we now refer to as *Doggerland*. And that's what became the poem.

41 In 2019, when my elder granddaughter was just 3 years old (and her sister was a baby) they and their parents visited my wife and I while we were staying in Goiânia, Brazil. The poem came out of that. Just before we left to return to the UK, I oiled both the swings and the see-saws, my small gift to local kids in the name of the promise to my granddaughter, leaving them functioning quietly, and better.

42 I've not written many poems about the changing seasons. This one is a sonnet.

43 Our minds become anaesthetised to the awfulness of much of the past, even the quite-recent past. Here, I attempt to liken our forgetfulness of horrors we once knew about, to the stunning fact that mankind does not even understand what makes up most of the universe. Again, it's in sonnet form. The 85% figure comes from *Wikipedia*. The Ukraine numbers, in the present context, are doubly shocking.

44 The theme of this poem fits with the previous one, *Oblivion*. My humanist world view is that mankind will be both happier and more prosperous when we finally comprehend that cooperation is best and that warfare, perpetrated almost entirely by men, is barbarous and inexcusable. End of. I yearn for the people of Ukraine to prevail in their struggle against Russia, which is currently ruled by a deranged psychopath. Sadly, the Russian people have never known freedom.

45 Published in *The Blue Nib,* #22, February 2018.

[46] *The translation of poetry is of the utmost importance, even though it is an impossibility.* - Edward Hirsch in *Poet's Choice.*

[47] In *Jorge Luis Borges - Selected Poems*, Penguin Books, 1999. Another example from the same book renders *enternecidas* as *eternal* instead of *tender* or *softened!* The best-informed remarks that I have seen on the trials and tribulations of translating poems are by Neil Astley, the redoubtable founding editor of *Bloodaxe Books*, who has commissioned vast amounts of poetry translation since 1987 (interviewed in *Poetry Salzburg Review*, # 40, 2023).

[48] Countess Emilia Pardo Bazán (1851-1921) was a Spanish novelist, journalist, literary critic, poet, playwright, translator, editor and professor. She introduced many feminist ideas, along with naturalism and descriptions of reality, making her one of the greatest and well-known female writers of her era. Her ideas about women's rights and education were important *(from Wikipedia).*

[49] My translation, from Portuguese, (re-lineated to fit the available space) was published by *Orbis* in its feature *Past Master*, together with the text shown below, with the permission of the poet's Trustees.

Cora Coralina was born Ana Lins dos Guimarães Peixoto in Goiás, central Brazil. Although her schooling was very limited, she was always a voracious reader and dreamed of becoming a writer. She adopted her literary name at age 15 and at 21 ran away, pregnant, with a married man to live in São Paulo. Her husband, by whom she had six children, would not allow her to publish her writings. He died in 1936 and after supporting the family on her own Cora finally returned to Goiás in 1956 where she earned her living selling home-made sweets and cakes. Her first poems were published only in 1965, at the age of 76. Carlos Drummond de Andrade, Brazil's most famous poet, read her second collection in 1979 and sent her a letter which the postal service managed to deliver although it bore no address. He said *I send these words on the wind, hoping that it will put them into your hands. I admire and love you as someone who lives in a state of grace with poetry,* and he praised her lyricism.

Cora then became a celebrity and politicians, academics and others wanted to associate with her.

[50] This is one of the poems I translated for the cover notes of the CD *De Un Tiempo a Esta Parte*, issued by Begoña Olavide and Javier Bergia. Antonio Machado (1875-1939) was a Spanish poet and a leading figures of the Spanish literary movement known as the Generation of '98. His work, initially modernist, evolved towards an intimate form of symbolism with romantic traits. He gradually developed a style characterised by both an engagement with humanity on the one hand and an almost Taoist contemplation of existence on the other, a synthesis that, according to Machado, echoed the most ancient popular wisdom. *(from Wikipedia)*

[51] Miguel Hernández (1910-1942) also featured in *De Un Tiempo a Esta Parte*. My translation was published in *Orbis* in its feature *Past Master*, together with the text that follows:

The poet and playwright was born in Alicante, Spain. Although he received little formal education he published some poems at the age of 23 and became quite well-known. His influences included the poets of the Spanish Golden Age and the Surrealists, who were fashionable during his formative years. However, he never abandoned formal poetic structures.

During the 1920s and 30s, a time of political tumult, he became active as a Republican and a member of the Communist Party. After the Spanish Civil War (1936-1939), he was arrested many times and received a death sentence, later commuted to 30 years of imprisonment. In jail, he continued writing poems before succumbing to ill-treatment and tuberculosis. In 2010, he was given a partial posthumous reprieve.

El Rayo Que No Cesa, here translated as *The Eternal Ray*, was published in 1936, as a sequence of 30 poems, mostly sonnets. Intricately rhymed, they are addressed to Hernández' lover. The poem shown is the 12th in the sequence. Translating it into a 'natural' English is a challenge, because English has far fewer rhymes than Spanish, and this particular sonnet has both internal and end rhymes.

[52] Javier Bergia is a living Spanish poet and musician. See his site at: www.javierbergia.com and Notes [33] and [50] above. This poem appears on Javier's CD *Divina Comedia* (Divine Comedy). I have slightly modified the published version of my translation to, I hope, improve it. Again, there is internal rhyme to deal with. Published with the permission of the poet.

[53] Miguel de Cervantes (1548-1616), was a Spanish novelist, playwright and poet, best known for his extraordinary novel *Don Quixote de la Mancha* published in two parts in 1605 and 1615.

[54] As of the date of writing, seven more of my poems have appeared in, or been accepted by other publications.